D0821564

A Book of Insects

Also by Charles Paul May
with illustrations by John Crosby

A Book of Canadian Animals
A Second Book of Canadian Animals
A Book of American Birds
A Book of Reptiles and Amphibians

A Book of
Insects

BY CHARLES PAUL MAY

ILLUSTRATIONS BY JOHN CROSBY

ST. MARTIN'S PRESS   NEW YORK
MACMILLAN OF CANADA   TORONTO

ISBN 0-7705-0758-1
Library of Congress Catalogue Card No. 72–83627

To Ethel K. Wilhelm, Margaret A. Webb,
and Edgerton G. Schoenhardt

Contents

Each chapter begins with a drawing of the fully-grown adult of the species. The drawing at the end shows the eggs or the young.

Introduction

Many of the animals you see every day have a backbone, a skull, ribs, leg bones, and other bones under their skins. The shape of every mammal, bird, reptile, and amphibian depends in part on its inside bone structure, or skeleton. Yet there are more animals without internal bones than there are with them. Those that you see most often are the insects.

The word "insect" comes from a Latin word that means "cut in". Look at a wasp or an ant. Its middle, often called the waist, looks as if it has been "cut in" so deeply that the body is almost divided in two.

Without an internal skeleton, what gives an insect its shape and holds it together? On its outside surface it wears a different kind of skeleton, a tough covering skin. This encloses many of its organs and systems – those for breathing, digesting, getting rid of waste products, and mating. Because the skeleton is outside the body instead of inside, we call this an exoskeleton. "Exo" is part of a Greek word meaning "outside".

Many insects are not "cut in" at all, yet they have

the same body divisions as those with narrow waists. At the front is the head, which contains the eyes, the mouth parts, and the antennae, or feelers. These organs show great variation in different types of insects, but since you need scientific instruments to study all the differences, only certain ones will be mentioned in the following chapters. They are often the ones you can see with the unaided eye or with a good magnifying glass.

It is perhaps desirable to mention the mandibles, however. These mouth parts correspond somewhat to jaws in other animals, but instead of holding teeth, they are sharp enough to do the cutting by themselves. And instead of working up and down like the jaws we know, they often open and close sideways. In insects that pierce the skin of other animals or plants, such as the mosquito, the mandibles have turned into sharp needles, or stylets, that are pushed forward to stab.

There may be two to four feeling organs around the mouth to help the insect know if it has found desirable food or where to use its mandibles. These palpi, or palps, are not the same as antennae.

Behind the head are three sections that make up one unit of the body – the thorax. It carries the legs and the wings. Every true insect has three pairs of legs (which tells you that spiders, with eight legs, and centipedes, with many more, are not insects and so will not be found in this book).

Each section of the thorax carries one pair of legs, and in most insects all six legs serve for walking or standing. The front segment of the thorax lacks wings. But in most insects that have wings, the middle and hind sections have one pair each. Flies are noteworthy for having only one pair of wings. Look at a fly and see if you can tell which thoracic segment of the two the wings are attached to.

The top part of the first thoracic section may grow like a cover, or shield, over the thorax. It may also cover part of an insect's head, or the insect may be able to pull its head partially back under this protective covering.

If an insect has a waist, it comes after the thorax. The connecting link between the thorax and the rest of the body is part of the rear end, or abdomen. Frequently, when people speak of an insect's body, they mean this abdominal part, which is usually made up of eleven sections. Outgrowths of the abdomen will be mentioned in some of the chapters but will not be mentioned for each insect. Attention will be called to them when they are especially noticeable.

The wings of one type of insect may differ considerably from those of another. Some fold, some

3

don't. Some are useless for flying, others are superb. When an insect flies, it doesn't just flap its wings up and down. It tilts the back edge up on the down stroke and down on the up stroke, at the same time moving them slightly forward or backward.

Legs, too, differ considerably. They usually consist of five sections, with a bendable joint between each section. Whereas a man's left knee always bends about the same as his right, a joint on an insect's front leg may bend differently from the corresponding joint on the middle or hind leg. Fortunately, an insect moves by instinct and doesn't have to think about what to do with each joint or leg segment. Instead of ending in a foot, an insect leg usually ends in claws, needed for climbing, crawling, or catching food.

When we speak of an insect with long legs, we mean in relation to the size of the rest of its body. A leg that would be short on a particularly large insect would be long if it grew from the thorax of a tiny one. So legs, wings, antennae, and other organs are large, or short, or medium when considered in relation to the size of the insect on which they occur.

The liquids inside an insect's body are not the same as the blood found in a mammal or a bird. For this reason they are often called juices or fluids, though referring to them as blood is not really wrong. These fluids change in temperature according to the temperature of the air around them. While your temperature stays about the same at all times, unless you are sick, that of the insect goes up and then down during the course of a day.

Like birds, nearly all insects develop from eggs. Very few insects give birth to living young. The various kinds of eggs all protect the young during their first few hours, days, or weeks of development outside the mother's body. Often the young that hatch from the eggs look like worms. These are called larvae.

Like adult insects, larvae have exoskeletons. In order to grow, larvae must develop new exoskeletons under the old ones. The new ones will be somewhat wet and wrinkled. After breaking or splitting out of the old skins, the young insects puff themselves up to expand the wrinkles of the new exoskeletons before they become dry and unmovable. Now they have a larger cover in which to grow. Each shedding of the old skin is known as a moult, and each time larvae want to get bigger they must go through the moulting process.

Finally, a larva must change into a real insect. It now goes into a period of rest, and ordinarily covers itself with some type of case, often a cocoon. At this stage the larva is called a pupa. Many changes occur to the pupa. The wings of the larva develop to full size and its legs and body become like those of an adult. When the larva breaks from the pupal covering, it is a fully grown insect. Ordinarily it will not moult any more and will stay the same size for the rest of its life. It will be sexually mature and able to reproduce its own kind.

Some young insects, however, come out of the eggs looking much like the adults except that they are smaller and lack wings. These young are usually called nymphs. They, too, moult again and again to grow larger and larger, but they do not go through the pupal stage. With their last moult, they emerge from the nymphal exoskeleton as adults.

Man lives in a state of constant warfare with insects. Many of these animals do cause damage and could make the problem of feeding the world's population more difficult than it is already if they were allowed to multiply unchecked. But in his fight against harmful insects, man often kills useful ones as well.

Don't go around killing insects just because you think they are all pests. Find out from this book and others which ones are helpful, and do what you can to keep those species alive.

Horse Fly

If a big black or blue-black fly about an inch long swoops about your head, stand still and swat at it. You'll probably miss, but you are more likely to hit it than you are to be able to run away from it. The horse fly can whiz along at six to ten miles an hour. To escape a wasp, it may fly more than twenty miles an hour.

When seeking a horse, cow, sheep, or deer, the female horse fly can cover fifty miles without stopping. She sees the world through large iridescent eyes that cover most of her wide head except for a narrow strip down the center. Each eye has hundreds and hundreds of tiny lenses, so it is called a compound eye. One lens sees only a small area, but the hundreds of images reaching the brain fit together to form a pattern of the fly's surroundings.

When something moves, the horse fly observes it closely. She speeds away if it is a bird that might catch her. But if it is a victim, she lands on its neck or some other spot where it cannot easily knock her off.

She has a stiff, tube-like mouth, called a proboscis. The proboscis has no teeth but it does have sharp parts for jabbing. With a forward thrust of her whole body, she stabs through the skin to get at the animal's blood. She needs this blood to feed the eggs that are developing in her body.

The male horse fly, needing no blood for eggs, feeds on the nectar and pollen in flowers. At mating time, in early summer, he flies into a clearing surrounded by trees and near water. Many males may occupy one clearing, but they keep their distance from one another as they hover and wait. When a female enters a male's territory, he swoops to catch her with his six legs, and they alight on a nearby plant. The male then fertilizes the female's eggs.

The female lays a mass of about a hundred eggs on a plant standing in or hanging over a quiet pool. In about a week the eggs hatch. The worm-like larvae drop into the water. They sink to the bottom of the pond and bury themselves in the mud. Here they eat other insects and small worms.

The larvae sleep through the winter, and in the spring they develop a pupal case. The fly's legs and wings had already started to develop under the larval skin after it hatched from the egg. Now, in the pupal stage, they grow out through the exoskeleton. Then the horsefly pupa must wriggle to the surface of the water at the edge of the pool in order to break from the pupal case.

Two short antennae stick forward from between the eyes of the fly. The wings are moist, but they slowly spread out and dry. They consist of filmy sections, somewhat smoky in colour, held together by stiff veins.

Behind the wings are two short rods that end in little knobs. Scientists call these halteres. A fly wiggles them when it flies, and they help the insect to fly smoothly.

The exoskeleton of the abdomen will be nearly black. Often in bright sunlight it appears bluish black.

These flies live mainly in eastern North America. However, black horse flies farther west differ only slightly from those of the east. They all fly by day and sleep at night. If one swoops around your head, you won't have time to worry about which species it is.

Mosquito

Have you ever counted the wings on a mosquito? You'll find two, for this animal belongs to the fly family. It is related to the horse fly, the house fly, the gnat, and the midge.

From north of the Arctic Circle to southern Florida, the mosquito slips through broken screens, open doors, and tent flaps. Active mainly at night, it can find you in complete darkness. Organs on its wiry front legs feel the heat from your body, guiding the mosquito to you.

After a mosquito lands, it settles parallel to your skin surface and then proceeds to cut it with the jagged edges of the mouth parts. It then inserts a thin tube into the opening it has created and injects a watery solution to dilute the blood. When the blood is the right consistency, it sucks it up.

When you kill one blood-sucking mosquito, you kill one hundred to four hundred of these insects. Only the female needs blood, which helps the eggs in her long, thin abdomen to develop. If you miss her, she in time seeks water standing in a pond, puddle, ditch, rain barrel, tin can, or hollow tree. She doesn't want it to be too fresh, as her babies eat tiny animals and plants in the water. Feeling the water with her antennae, she judges if it is satisfactory.

She quickly lays one egg after another. They stick together, forming a raft of up to four hundred eggs. Once the eggs are laid, in May or June, the mother will die two to four weeks later.

The eggs hatch in one to three days. The larvae, called wrigglers, look like brown or reddish sticks made up of about a dozen sections. On the next to last section, a little tube, or siphon, sticks up. The larvae breathe through this tube by pushing it up through the surface of the water.

If a shadow falls across the water, the larvae use leaf-like paddles on the ends of their tails to wriggle to the bottom. As soon as danger passes, they return to the surface, although they can stay under about ten minutes, if necessary.

Mosquito larvae must escape fish, water insects, birds, and the larvae of dragonflies and damsel flies. If they do, they grow for a week or two and develop into pupae. A pupa has a bulging front section, which contains the head and the thorax, but the abdomen remains slender. Pupae go without food, but unlike the pupae of most other insects they continue to move about. They rise to the surface to breathe through two tiny tubes on the back of the thorax, and they squirm away from danger. They are called tumblers.

After two or three days, the pupal case splits open. Males step out into the air first. Their wings quickly spread and dry, and in about three minutes an adult mosquito flies. It flaps its wings about three hundred times a second and travels at a rate of three to five miles an hour. It must watch out for flycatchers, nighthawks, swallows, robber flies, damsel flies, and dragonflies.

The females hatch half a day to a day later. When they fly, their wings make a buzzing sound. The males have bushy, or feathery, antennae with which they "hear" this buzzing by receiving the vibrations from it. After mating takes place, both the male and the female feed on plant nectar. In about a week, the male dies and the female starts her search for blood.

Man kills mosquitoes whenever possible because mosquitoes can carry many harmful diseases. Unfortunately, man also kills other animals, such as birds, when powerful insecticides are used. The most effective way of getting rid of mosquitoes is to destroy their breeding places by draining still and stagnant water.

Bumble Bee

A warm day in early spring brings out a thick-bodied yellow and black bee an inch or so long. She seems to bumble along as she flies a zigzag course low over the ground. Actually, she is on a search. Seeing an old mouse hole, she enters. If a tunnel one to six feet long leads to a chamber, she may take this as her nesting place.

Watch for bumble bees across southern Canada and throughout the United States below the Canadian border. The greatest number live in Manitoba and Ontario and through the midwest of the United States.

As she starts her nest, the bumble bee queen has no helpers. She puts down a pad of leaves and grass on which to build a bowl of brown wax. She fills it with pollen which she has carried on her hind legs where long hairs form a sort of basket. In May or June she lays six to twelve eggs in the pollen.

Over the eggs the queen spreads a cap of wax. To provide extra warmth, she lies on top of the bowl. She leaves the nest only for hasty meals of pollen and nectar and to bring nectar to the chamber. In another cup, or "honey pot", she builds up a food supply.

The eggs hatch in about four days, and the larvae eat the pollen around them. The queen breaks a small hole in the bowl to feed them more pollen and honey. About seven days later, each larva wraps itself in a cocoon.

A pupa remains in its cocoon at least eleven days. During this time, the queen opens the top of the bowl. After biting through its cocoon, a young bee crawls to the "honey pot" and feeds. Soon it returns to the warmth under the queen, but in a couple of days its hairy coat fluffs out and it starts helping with the work.

The first young are all workers. Workers are females that lack the ability to lay eggs. They spend their short lives helping with the queen's next eggs and young.

Small enemies, such as ants, mice, or shrews, may come down the tunnel. In the rear segment of its abdomen, a bumble bee has a stinger connected to two poison sacs. The venom can kill a mouse if a bee stings it a few times.

Bigger enemies – foxes, skunks, bears, or badgers – dig into the nest to eat the honey and the young.

The queen, even with helpers, may be unable to drive these foes away.

The worst enemy is man. He kills bumble bees with poisons meant for other insects, and he ploughs up grasslands where the bees nest. Man, himself, is the loser. In gathering nectar, bumble bees spread pollen from flower to flower and thereby fertilize the plants. A plant that is not fertilized cannot produce seeds that will grow.

After two months of producing workers, the queen has grown old. In the last month of her laying period, she lays eggs from which male bees emerge. Like the workers, they are half her size. They fly from the nest and never return.

The queen's last eggs produce fertile females which are large queens like herself. Before long they fly away. These new queens attract the males by the sweet odour they give off, and after mating they will eat and get ready for winter. Queen bumble bees hibernate during the cold weather by burrowing into the soil. They will start new colonies in the spring.

The males, their work done, die during chilly days. The old queen and her workers have also finished their jobs and fall asleep, never to wake again.

Don't run from bumble bees. They are good-natured and attack only when in danger.

Carpenter Ant

Have you ever mistaken an ant for a bumble bee? Probably not, yet they are close relatives and often live similar lives. If you see an ant flying you might mistake it for a wasp, which is another relative. Most ants, bees, and wasps are social insects. This means they live and work together in colonies, or groups.

Among the most common and largest ants in the United States and Canada are black carpenter ants. We call them carpenters because they live in wood. They gnaw into logs, stumps, fence posts, and telephone poles. Sometimes they tunnel into healthy trees and injure them. Worse still, they may burrow into the beams or walls of buildings.

Termites also live in wood, but ants differ from termites. Termites swallow and digest wood. Carpenter ants do not eat wood, but leave a trail of sawdust wherever they burrow. The ants are dark to shiny black in colour, while termites may be nearly white. Ants have jointed antennae. Ants also have a very thin waist connecting the thorax to the abdomen. Although it looks like a separate section, the waist is the first segment of the abdomen. One hump, or node, sticks up on the waist of the carpenter ant.

As in a bee colony, an ant nest has many workers. Most of the carpenters you see will be workers. Some may be soldiers. Like the workers, they are females that cannot produce eggs, and they defend the nest from enemies.

Unlike a bee society, more than one queen ant may live in a nest. The carpenter queens reach a length of about an inch while the workers are only half an inch long.

Young carpenter ants go through larval and pupal stages similar to those of the bumble bee, but each stage may last a few days longer. The larvae are white, legless grubs with a thin pointed head and a fat body.

Carpenter ants eat other small insects or steal sweet foods from your kitchen. The workers digest the food in their own bodies, then cough some of it up to feed the larvae.

At certain periods, the queens lay eggs that produce other queens and also males. These ants have wings. For a time, these queens and males remain in the nest.

Soon there will come a day when the sun shines warm and bright, and when little or no wind blows.

As if at a secret signal, the new queens and males from all the nests in a region take to the air. This is the mating flight.

Shortly after mating, the males die. The queens land on the ground, bite or rub off their wings, and seek places to start new colonies. Like the bumble bee queen starting out in the spring, the new ant queen must do all the work at first. She lays only a few eggs, which will produce workers to help her.

A carpenter ant queen may live ten to fifteen years. She remains fertile all that time, although she mates only during that one flight before she removes her wings.

Carpenters live across southern Canada and throughout the United States. The black carpenter ant can be found in great numbers east of the Mississippi River. Don't be afraid to watch it, just don't pick it up. If handled, the carpenter ant bites hard.

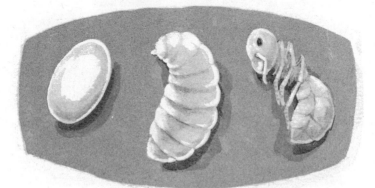

Bald-faced Hornet

Most wasps have hairless or almost hairless faces. This one has a yellow to whitish head except for a black strip across the top. Since its face looks especially bare, it is called the bald-faced hornet. Another name is white-faced hornet.

The sides of the thorax and the end segments of the abdomen also show yellow. Most of the rest of the body is black.

This wasp stings again and again to defend itself or its nest. Some wasps sting to kill food, but not the bald-faced hornet. It sinks its mandibles into the victim's neck or head.

The hornet eats caterpillars, nectar, and fruit juices. When it catches caterpillars that eat garden vegetables, it aids man. But when it bites into ripe fruit, it causes damage. In the long run, it does more good than harm and should be left alone.

In the spring, a hornet queen wings among trees and bushes seeking a place to nest. On the plains east of the Rocky Mountains where few trees grow, she may build under the eaves of a building. The largest number of bald-faced hornets occupy wooded areas in the eastern half of the United States and southern Canada.

Once she has found a nesting place, the queen seeks a dead limb, a rotting stump, or an old weather-worn tree. She bites off wood to chew, mixing it with her saliva. She pastes the pulp to the spot where she wants her nest to hang. While the pulp remains moist, she forms it into a thin sheet. It dries and becomes solid. We call it paper.

The queen hornet adds more pulp to the thin edge of the first mouthful. Each time she adds more pulp she works it into a thin sheet that extends the paper cover. In time she has an oval about the size of a hen's egg.

Inside the cover, the bald-faced queen builds a few cells. They hang down, so the queen must paste each egg to the inside of a cell. When an egg hatches, the larva secretes a substance that enables it to stick to the paper.

The queen chews caterpillars and other insects into soft wads. She feeds these to her larvae, which grow until each one fills its cell. Then it wraps itself in a cocoon of silk.

The queen makes the nest larger by building an-other cover over the first. When the pupae become adult hornets, they are all workers. They help enlarge the nest, leaving the queen more time for laying eggs.

After adding outside covers to the nest, the hornets tear out the inner layers of paper. Thus they make the inside larger. But they add more covers than they remove, so the nest grows stronger and better protected from heat or cold. With more room inside, the hornets build more rows of cells. By the end of summer, the nest may be ten to twenty inches across and have several tiers of cells.

Late in summer, the workers build extra-large cells. In these, the queen lays eggs that will become the future queens. She also lays eggs that will produce drones, or males.

After they mate, the males die. The new queens eat and find places in which to pass the winter. The old queen stops laying, and cold weather brings an end to life in the paper nest.

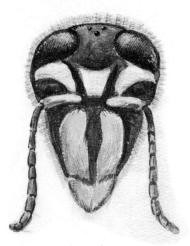

American Painted Lady

The American painted lady is a butterfly. Can you tell a butterfly from a moth?

A butterfly usually has a slender body. A moth is likely to have a thick thorax and perhaps a thick abdomen. The bodies of moths often look furry, while those of butterflies do not. The antennae of butterflies resemble threads except at the tips, where they swell into knobs. Antennae of moths do not have knobs at the end.

If you see one of these insects flying in broad daylight, it will most likely be a butterfly. Moths usually fly at night.

You will find the American painted lady throughout the first forty-eight states of the United States except near the Canadian border in the northwest. In Canada, look for it everywhere east of the Rockies and as far north as the Northwest Territories.

The body of the American painted lady will be a bit less than an inch long. The wings will spread out to about two inches.

This butterfly is reddish brown with whitish spots

at the corners of its triangular front wings. Near the middle of these wings are dark blotches.

On the back wings, the American painted lady has black strips along the outer edge. Just in from the outer edge, it has four round bluish dots.

Tiny scales cover the wings and give them their colour. The front wings of butterflies overlap the back wings so that they move together. Butterflies have an irregular, up and down flight.

As a rule, a female American painted lady produces two sets of young a year. In the far north, the second group may sleep in their pupal cases through the winter. In the far south, a female may have more than two broods.

She lays the eggs in small groups on the leaves of cudweed, arrowroot and forget-me-not. The leaves of these plants serve as food for the larvae, or caterpillars, when they hatch.

Each butterfly has its own type of caterpillar. The caterpillar of the American painted lady has a black exoskeleton that looks like velvet. From the back of each segment, short black spikes stick up, and there is a yellow to red band across the back of each section. This caterpillar has a row of white dots along each side.

The caterpillar spins a nest of silk. When it enters the pupal stage, it crawls into its nest and sheds its last larval skin. It now wears a hard pupal covering. At this point, it is called a chrysalis.

When the butterfly emerges, its wings look crumpled. As they unfold and dry in the sun, they stand up straight.

Although insects have six legs, the American painted lady belongs to a group known as four-footed butterflies. The front legs are so short, they are almost useless.

This butterfly eats nectar and pollen. Curled under its chin it carries a very long proboscis through which it feeds.

Some people collect butterflies. As they flit about, these insects offer a challenge to the collector. But if it is a challenge you want, try photographing them. Successful pictures will give you the colour of the butterfly without cheating the rest of the world of its beauty.

Cecropia Moth

A big name for a big moth. The ancient Greeks told a legend that a creature named Cecrops built Athens. Half man, half snake, he supposedly sprang from the soil. He called his city Cecropia, before it became Athens.

In the larval stage, the Cecropia moth looks somewhat like a small serpent. For a caterpillar, it is large, being about four inches long. On its light green or blue-green body stand rows of club-like knobs, or tubercles.

The caterpillar spins a cocoon of brown silk when it enters the pupal stage in late summer. The cocoon is thick in the middle and tapers toward each end. Although it is sometimes found under leaves, it can also be fastened to a twig or branch in an elm, maple, cherry, apple, pear, or willow tree. The caterpillar eats the leaves of the tree before it starts to pupate.

The adult emerges the following May or June. As its wings dry in the sun, they stand straight over the Cecropia's back. Most moths hold their wings like a shield over their bodies, but this moth holds its wings up as butterflies do.

The Cecropia's wings are reddish brown to dull red near the body and out past the centres. Beyond the centre, a broad, wavy white stripe runs from the forward edge to the back edge of each wing. The outer edges may be greyish or yellowish. Near the centre of each wing is a kidney-shaped light spot that is so thin you can see through it. Toward the forward outside corner of each front wing, a large black spot looks a bit like an eye. A small bird, seeing those eye-like spots, might be frightened away, but not owls, thrashers, or woodpeckers. Woodpeckers and blue jays also peck their way into the tough cocoons and eat the pupae.

The wings of the Cecropia moth spread five to six inches, and the bodies are an inch or more long. These are the largest moths in Canada and the United States. Look for them east of the Rocky Mountains, but not as far north as James Bay or as far south as the southern end of Florida.

A Cecropia has a thick, furry red thorax. The abdomen, also red, tapers to a blunt end and has white stripes around it.

The antennae look like feathers. They contain tiny pits through which the insect senses odours. After the female emerges from the chrysalis, she gives off a scent that males pick up five or more miles away if the wind carries it in their direction.

Mating takes place shortly before the sun comes up. Afterwards, the female seeks the right leaves on which to lay her eggs. She usually lays one at a time, though she may place a few in groups. They look like little buns.

As days pass, the adults grow weak. They do not eat, but live on fat stored in their bodies the summer before when they were caterpillars. They can survive for only a week or ten days.

In Asia, relatives of the Cecropia moth produce silk used for cloth. In North America, the silk has been tried for fishing lines but not for cloth. The Cecropia caterpillar does not spin a single long thread but produces many short ones. Since the strand varies in thickness, it is hard to handle.

The main thing the Cecropia offers us is beauty. If you see one flying by day, it is probably a male. Females, like males and females of most moth families, come out at night.

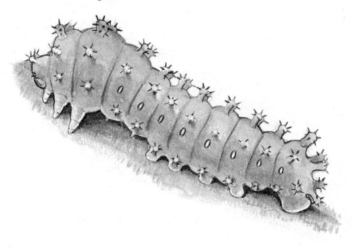

Carolina Grasshopper

Clackety-clackety-clackety-clack. A brown insect about two inches long leaps into the air as you walk along the side of a dusty road. On fan-shaped black wings with yellow margins, it rattles away from you.

You have just frightened a Carolina grasshopper. Some hoppers fly only when you get very close, but the Carolina takes to the air rather quickly.

If it is a nymph – a young one without wings – it leaps away from danger. Grasshoppers have long hind legs with strong muscles, and the Carolina can jump for a distance of two to three feet. It may land on its side, but its light weight and strong exoskeleton save it from harm.

The Carolina's brown body is spotted with grey and red. Between the eyes stand short antennae, which give it the common name of short-horned grasshopper. Locust is another name for a grasshopper.

A sort of shield covers the thorax, and when the insect rests, its front wings cover the back ones. In fact, the back ones are the only ones a grasshopper uses in flying. The narrow front wings act as stiff shields to protect the back ones when they aren't in use.

From the Rocky Mountains east, and especially in southern Canada and the United States east of the Mississippi River, the Carolina grasshopper lives in pastures and fields. It eats some corn, wheat, oats, rye, and other grasses raised by man, feasting by day and resting at night. Several other grasshoppers do far more damage, but the Carolina suffers with the rest when farmers put out poisons or spray with insect killers. Ploughing land to expose the eggs to weather and enemies is one way to control grasshoppers, but it never kills all of them.

In May or June, the grasshopper nymph crawls out of the ground. Its head looks much too large for the small body, and it lacks wings. Its strong mandibles have sharp grinding surfaces and it starts to eat immediately. Its hind legs are well developed, helping it to leap away from skunks, toads, snakes, lizards, turtles, shrews, and birds, especially sparrow hawks.

During the next five to eight weeks it sheds its exoskeleton five or six times. Its wings grow from tiny bumps, or wing buds, but they are not usable until the nymph moults for the last time.

Grown grasshoppers make more noise than most other insects. The male scrapes the thick part of his hind legs against the veins of his wings to produce a dr-r-r-r-r-r sound. A female picks up the sound on large sense organs, one on each side of the first segment of her abdomen. If still a nymph, she pays no attention. If she is an adult nearly ready to lay eggs, she answers.

When the male and female draw near each other, the male changes the sound to a courting "song". Perhaps another male also courts her. The males then have a "song battle", until one loses interest and goes away. If they take too long, the female also loses interest and goes to answer some other male's call.

After she mates, the female ignores all males. With prong-like organs on the end of her abdomen, she digs into the ground. Her abdomen is longer than the male's, for the rear section is made up of the ovipositor, or egg-laying organ. She pushes this an inch into the ground and lays a group of about fifty eggs.

By the time she lays, late summer or early fall has arrived. A good frost kills her and all other adults. If mice, moles, insects in the ground, and man leave them alone, the eggs will hatch the following year.

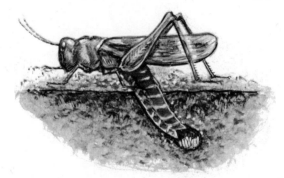

Field Cricket

"Greh-greh-greh". Or perhaps to you it sounds like "cree-cree-cree". To some people this "song" sounds like "cree-keet". Long ago, someone tried to express the sound with a human word and invented the name "cricket". Crickets are close relatives of grasshoppers, katydids, praying mantises, walkingsticks, and cockroaches.

During summer, the field cricket lives outdoors, eating ordinary grass, wheat, oats, lettuce, tomatoes, peas, or strawberries. It also eats small insects, and will even devour another cricket. With the arrival of fall, this black or dark brown insect may enter your house. If you hear it chirping in the clothes closet, get it out before it feeds on your garments.

The field cricket looks like a small grasshopper, being about three-fourths of an inch long. However, the cricket has a rounded body, while the grasshopper is long and thin.

The field cricket has two thread-like antennae as long as, or longer than, its body. Two thin rods stand up on the cricket's back near the end of the abdomen. These cerci may look to you like stiff, misplaced antennae. In a way they are, for through them the cricket senses vibrations in the air or along the ground. Grasshoppers and many other insects also have cerci, often so short you do not see them as easily as you do those on the field cricket.

Cerci do not take the place of ears. The cricket "hears" sounds through organs on its first pair of legs.

Sounds of interest to field crickets are chirpings of other field crickets. On each front wing, this insect has a roughened area, like a tiny file. Also on each front wing it grows a small scraper. By bringing the scraper of one wing across the file of the other, the field cricket "sings".

The male does the chirping. As with grasshoppers, the warmer the weather the more actively a cricket "sings". But if two male field crickets are near the same female, they do not battle with "music". They attack each other. One may lose a leg or even his life.

Field crickets seldom fly. They do so to escape enemies, but they are more likely to take long leaps. In seeking food, the cricket walks, runs, or hops.

Crickets and grasshoppers have four short sensing organs around their mouths to aid them in finding food. With these palpi, or palps, the insects can tell if something can be eaten. The field cricket often holds food in its front feet, like a squirrel with a nut be-tween its paws.

The field cricket has a life cycle similar to that of the Carolina grasshopper. After mating, the female pushes her needle-like ovipositor into the ground and lays eggs, usually in groups. She lays about three hundred before the cold weather kills her.

The eggs hatch in May or early June. The nymphs take about a month longer than those of the grasshopper to mature. During this time, the crickets moult their exoskeletons about twice as many times as the Carolina hoppers do.

Unlike grasshoppers, field crickets rest by day and become active at night. Before going to rest, a cricket cleans itself. It uses its legs and its mandibles to scrape dirt from its body. Then it settles under a rock, a log, or a board, where it has dug a little hollow.

For centuries, field crickets have been kept as pets, but with patience you can study them outdoors. Except on high mountain slopes or north of the Arctic Circle, these insects live all over the North American continent.

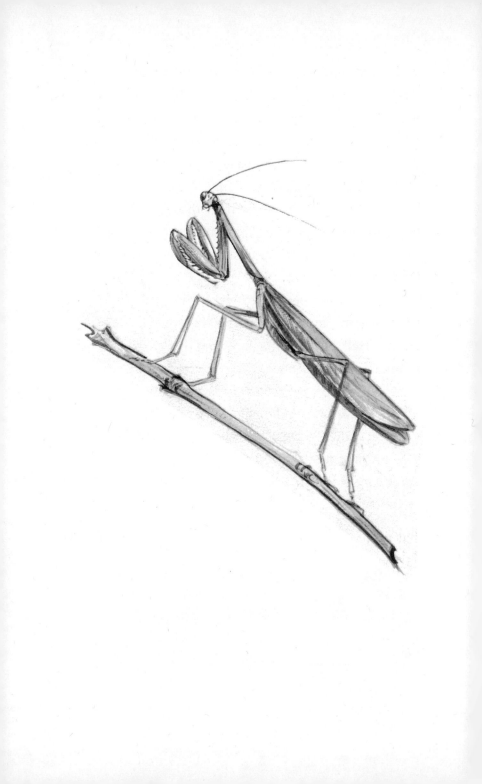

Praying Mantis

Crickets leap; bees fly through the air; yet one of our slowest insects catches them.

The praying mantis stalks prey so leisurely, you hardly notice that the stick-like legs move. Or else it stands motionless and lets rushing insects come to it. By being slow, the mantis escapes being seen.

Its colour also makes the praying mantis hard to notice. Because its green and brown coat blends with leaves and twigs, many animals fail to see it. Small birds leave this fierce insect alone, but large birds can kill it.

When it does travel, the mantis walks on four legs. To take a step, most insects move the front and hind legs on one side and the middle leg on the other. This leaves the animals a firm tripod of the other three legs on which to balance. Not the mantis. It uses its front legs for catching food, not for walking.

As it waits for insect victims, a mantis holds its stout front legs folded near its head. To some people it resembles a human saying a prayer. This is why it has been named the praying mantis.

The front legs shoot forward like released springs and clamp together on a victim. Sharp spines on the legs hold the prey fast. The mantis pulls the struggling prisoner to its small, triangular-shaped head and bites the victim in the neck.

The praying mantis is a large insect measuring three inches in length. The thorax is long and slender, like a stick, while the abdomen is thicker.

The wings fold along the back, reaching the tip of the abdomen. Although it seldom flies, this insect uses all four wings. You can almost see through the thin wings.

Males seek mates in August or early September. While mating, the female may turn, grab and start to eat the male. It does not matter, for autumn will kill them both.

Around a twig, the female squirts a whitish froth from her abdomen. Within this foam she lays about three hundred eggs. As it dries, the froth forms a hard brown cover.

The case keeps the eggs from freezing, whether in southern Ontario and Quebec or on south throughout the eastern United States. But if woodpeckers or mice break in, they eat the eggs.

Warm days in spring soften the egg case. The

nymphs wriggle out, but a thin, sac-like cover still holds each one prisoner. This sac dangles by a silken thread. At this stage, they are tasty food for ants or birds.

Breaking free of its sac, the pale yellow nymph crawls up the thread. Within twenty minutes its exoskeleton hardens and it starts to hunt.

Catch a praying mantis and it turns its head as if to see what holds it. The mantis may be the only insect able to twist its neck around to look down its back.

A captured mantis can spit out a brown fluid, as the Carolina grasshopper does. This mistakenly named "tobacco juice" is harmless. Perhaps it causes some birds to drop their prey.

The praying mantis was not brought from Europe purposely to catch harmful insects. It came as an uninvited guest, riding on some plants. After arriving, it spread, moving slowly, as always.

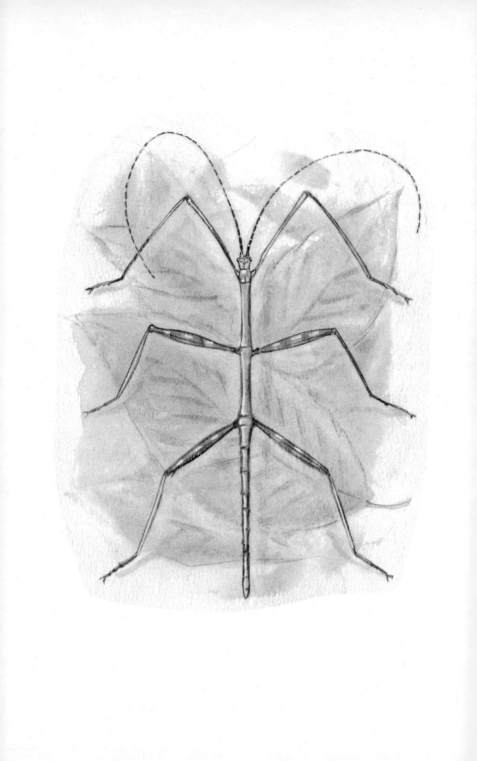

Walkingstick

How long can you stand in one spot without moving? The common walkingstick can do it from sunrise to sundown. Not only can do it, but does it, day after day for the course of one summer.

The walkingstick may be even slower than the praying mantis, for it never needs to shoot out its front legs to catch anything. Instead, it dines on leaves. It lives in black locust, walnut, hickory, wild cherry, or oak trees. It feeds at night, and with the coming of the dawn it rests.

As the walkingstick stands on a leaf or limb, its greyish to brownish green exoskeleton blends with the background. Grackles and other birds, lizards, mice, and praying mantises frequently miss out on a meal of walkingstick. Its colour and its ability to stay still hour after hour save its life.

If an enemy comes near, it has little chance of escape, for it isn't a fighter like its relative the praying mantis.

In some ways, the common walkingstick resembles

the mantis. Both insects have long, stick-like middle and hind legs. Their front legs differ considerably, however. The mantis has grasping front legs that are thicker and shorter than the other two pairs. The walkingstick has thin front legs similar to its other two pairs.

Both insects have thin thoraxes. But the walkingstick has a small, rounded head rather than a triangular one, and a thin abdomen. While the mantis has large, globe-like eyes, the stick insect has small sight organs set into the sides of its face.

Especially noticeable is the absence of wings on the walkingstick. It has antennae that are much longer and more thread-like than those of the mantis.

The walkingstick produces no "song". It has no need to. The female can lay fertile eggs without ever mating, so neither sex needs to call the other. If you see a walkingstick, it will probably be a female. The males are shorter and more difficult to see. They are also rare.

In late spring, walkingstick nymphs hatch from small eggs that have lain on the ground all winter, protected only by their hard shells and by fallen leaves. The young go through five or six moults to become adults. If a nymph loses a leg, it grows a new one, or part of one, under its next skin. When it moults again, this new leg will be usable.

In late summer, the mature female can lay about a hundred eggs. Instead of seeking a special place for them, she walks along the underside of a limb and lets them drop to the ground one at a time. Where walkingsticks live near one another and several lay at the same time, the eggs falling on dry leaves sound like a light rain.

Adult walkingsticks change colour. By the time the first heavy frost in fall ends their lives, they will be more yellow than green.

Some walkingsticks can be found in the southwestern United States and as far west as the California coast. They are most common in all states east of the Rockies. Southern Florida lacks the common stick but has instead a close relative.

In Canada, one species of walkingstick can be found in southern Manitoba, southern and central Ontario and Quebec, and the Maritimes.

Ladybug Beetle

Ladybug, ladybug,
Fly away home!
Your house is on fire;
Your children will burn.

This rhyme comes from England, where the burning of hop vines once forced ladybugs to take to the air. The name "ladybug", or "ladybird", also originated in Europe, though on the Continent rather than in England. Because the beetles did so much good, farmers dedicated them to the mother of Christ – "Our Lady".

From this, we can guess that ladybugs, sometimes called lady beetles, are found in many places. As a matter of fact, they live all over the world. All parts of the United States have them, and they can be found from coast to coast across Canada. The most common one, the two-spotted ladybug, makes its home in the eastern provinces and states.

The two-spotted ladybug has a bright red "back" with a black spot on each side. This "back" is actually the wing covers, which come together to completely hide the top of the abdomen. The thorax is also hidden by a cover, and this almost hides the head as well.

These coverings fit together to give the beetle a round shape. The back is arched, while the belly is flat, causing the ladybug to look like half a ball when seen from the side.

On short legs ending in claws, the beetle crawls over leaves. Short antennae end in knobs. When the two-spotted ladybug stretches its head forward to catch a mite or an aphid, you will see it has two large eyes bulging out from the tiny face.

Though the two-spotted ladybug is small – a fourth to a third of an inch long – its bright colour may attract enemies. But it has ways to protect itself. For one thing, it may play dead. It also squeezes a fluid from the joints of its legs and from the thorax where the wings grow. The disagreeable odour of this blood-like juice usually drives attackers away.

The lady beetle, in turn, is a killer. It eats aphids, scale insects, potato beetle eggs, and mites. In doing so, it saves many important food and flower plants from damage.

Both adult and larvae ladybugs feed on small insects. The larvae seem to eat all day, though they undoubtedly rest at night just as the adults do. A larva has a wide thorax. Each segment of the abdomen is smaller than the one ahead of it, giving the young insect a tapered look. It is grey to purplish spotted with black, brown, blue, or red.

When ready to shed its larval cover for the fourth time, the immature insect glues itself to the underside of a leaf. The exoskeleton splits, and the young one may wriggle to slide the old cover up around its abdomen. Then the pupa hangs head down until it turns into an adult.

During a summer, an adult female lays about two hundred eggs. She may place each one individually, sticking it to a leaf, or she may lay a few together.

As fall arrives, the adults gather together in groups, perhaps thousands of them collecting on one rock or log. They hibernate, or sleep through the winter, under loose bark on a tree, in piles of leaves, or under logs and rocks. Some may enter houses to find warm wintering places.

People who believe in good luck signs often think a ladybug in the house will bring good fortune. But the place where it really brings good fortune is in the vegetable garden, flower bed, or orchard.

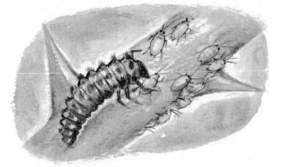

Firefly

The firefly has four wings. Since flies have only two, we see at once that the firefly is not a fly at all. It also goes by the name lightning bug, but it is not a true bug either. Like the ladybug, it is a beetle.

In beetles, the front wings play little part in flying. They form a shield for the folded rear wings and the abdomen when the beetles are not in the air. The front wings of fireflies are usually black or brown and the triangular rear ones are tan, yellowish, or grey.

Fireflies are not fast flyers. They remain in one area, often a damp region near a pool, stream, or dew-coated lawn. Here they seek mates by flashing signals.

In the last sections of its abdomen, the male firefly can produce a heatless light. The female can do the same in one segment near the end of her abdomen.

The signalling segments are made up of fatty tissues which contain a system of air channels. Substances formed in the tissues come together and, in the presence of oxygen from the air, glow briefly. The length and the colour of the glow depend on the species. The common fireflies of the United States and Canada give off yellowish lights.

In Canada, fireflies occur mainly in southern Ontario, southern Quebec, and the Maritime Provinces. In the United States, you can find them throughout the eastern half of the country and across the southwest to the Pacific coast. Darkness brings them out from under leaves and the bark of trees, where they rest by day.

Among our most interesting lightning bugs are those known as glow-worms. You will need to be in the east to see them. From southern Maine to central North Carolina and west through Indiana they can be found in damp, grassy areas. Canada has them in southern Ontario.

Among the glow-worms, females have such short wings that they are called wingless and are unable to fly. The males show an up, down, up, down flight pattern. Each time they start up, they light their cold fires. If a female recognizes the light as being from a male of her species, she flashes about two seconds later. Her light is weak, but since the male has big, bulging eyes, much larger than hers, he can see her answering signal. He heads in her direction, still flashing at regular periods. She answers regularly until he lands near her.

The female lays tiny eggs in or on the ground, or

in beds of moss. The broad larvae hatch in about three weeks, and in another three weeks they can produce a light.

Worms, snails, and the larvae of other small insects fall prey to young lightning bugs. Firefly larvae, about half an inch long, can kill animals much larger than themselves. When they bite, a fluid from their mandibles paralyzes the victim.

Adult male fireflies probably do not eat, and live for only a few days or weeks. Some females may not eat, but the glow-worm species sometimes does. If a male firefly of the wrong kind lands near her, the adult female glow-worm will eat him. She may even flash her light on the right schedule to attract him to his death.

Adult fireflies die before summer ends. The larvae sleep through winter in the ground or in rotting logs or stumps of trees. With the arrival of spring, they enter the pupal stage and then become adults.

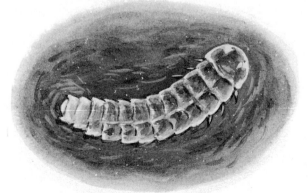

June Bug

Like ladybugs and lightning bugs, June bugs are really beetles. You can see as many in May as you can in June, so don't be surprised if you hear them called May beetles. Common species in North America occur in all states and provinces.

The farmer and the forest ranger wage war against the June bug. The adult insects eat the leaves of elm, oak, and poplar. Several bugs on one small tree can strip it of foliage.

The larvae chew the roots of corn, oats, wheat, and other grasses, or may turn to other plants if grasses prove scarce. Ploughing fields in fall helps get rid of June bugs, for birds then find the larvae easily and chilly weather kills them.

Natural enemies of June bugs include crows and other large birds that can peck or scratch them out of the ground or catch them in the air. Since the adult beetles fly mainly at night, they escape being seen by most birds. Skunks dig up the larvae, and pigs may root them out. An unusual enemy is a fly.

The *Pyrgota* fly cannot attack the June bug when it is on the ground. As with other beetles, the June bug has tough front wings that protect its flying wings and its body while it rests. Once the beetle takes to the air, however, the *Pyrgota* fly dives onto the June bug's back. Quickly the fly shoves an egg into the soft tissue of the beetle's abdomen. The June bug continues its life of eating leaves and storing up food in its body.

After the fly egg hatches, the *Pyrgota* larva eats the food supply built up in the beetle's body. As a result, the beetle dies. Its parasite continues to live in the beetle's abdomen.

Since the beetle can no longer supply food, it is time for the immature fly to pupate. As a pupa it passes the winter, finally leaving the beetle's body as an adult *Pyrgota* fly the following spring.

The female June bug lays her eggs on the ground where plants of the grass family grow. She covers them with soil. When the larvae hatch, they burrow down among the roots and start to feed. They are plump, whitish, somewhat hairy creatures about an inch long, known as white grubs. They remain in the earth for two or three summers.

At the end of their larval life, they pupate before winter. The pupal stage ends the following spring, when the inch-long adults crawl from the ground.

A mature June bug has reddish brown to brownish yellow front wings. Its shield is the same colour. Its belly is hairy, and the long, thin legs carry spiky hairs. The antennae, which end in knobs, are very small.

Bright lights attract June bugs. With a low hum they smash into street lamps or bang against the screen windows of houses.

The low hum tells you that these leisurely moving insects have fairly slow wing beats. They beat their wings about forty-five times a second. The bumble bee, with a higher pitch to its buzz, has a rhythm of about a hundred and thirty, while the high whine of a mosquito comes from around three hundred beats every second.

Dog Flea

If you ever want a model for a monster in a horror story, look at a dog flea through a magnifying glass. It appears to have a hooded face, with only the small eyes showing. Two palpi and a row of bristles hang under the face. Other bristles stick out all over the long legs and the strange body, which is very thin from side to side but thick from top to bottom. The legs end in long, sharp claws.

You may feel a dog flea before you see one. Less than a quarter of an inch long, fleas often escape being seen. You may get bitten because they eat the blood of people as well as of dogs or cats.

If you develop swellings that itch, try not to scratch them. The flea often drops wastes where it has fed. If you scratch these into the bite, you might cause an infection.

In parts of the world, fleas spread serious diseases, but this seldom happens in Canada and the United States. Dog fleas of North America live wherever there are dogs.

Fleas are parasites. This means they live on or make use of other animals for survival. The *Pyrgota* fly that lays its egg in the June bug's abdomen is also a parasite. Fleas are not members of the fly family, but form a separate group. However, scientists think that long ago, the closest relatives of fleas may have been flies.

The shape of the dog flea is quite suitable for its way of life. Because it is so thin from side to side, the flea does not get wedged between the hairs on a dog's body. And it has no wings to become entangled.

You may think the flea lacks antennae. Actually, these tiny organs are in grooves on the sides of a flea's face. They help the flea to avoid getting caught in the hairy jungle on a dog.

Away from its host – the animal on which it lives – the flea covers ground in a hurry. Its hind legs are especially long and in one spring it may sail eight inches up into the air and land a foot from where it started. Oddly enough, the jumping legs flip it over. Instead of going head first, it turns a somersault.

An adult flea has needle-like mouth parts to pierce the skin, and it has siphons, or tubes, through which to suck blood. It feeds often but can go for weeks without food if it has to.

The female lays her eggs in the dog's hair, but they drop off into the dog's bed or onto the floor or ground. In about two weeks, the larva, with the aid of a sharp spike on its head, cuts through the eggshell.

The whitish larva lives on many types of food. It finds minute substances in dust or in the fuzz of rugs. If the wastes of adult fleas are at hand, it can live on the blood in those. Adult fleas do not digest food very well, so undigested blood remains in the droppings.

When food is plentiful and the weather warm, a larva may pupate in a week or so. If conditions are poor, it takes many weeks to enter the pupal stage. It spins a cocoon around itself and looks a bit like a tiny button.

The speed with which a pupa develops also depends on temperature. In hot days, the brown to blackish adult may emerge in about a week; in cold weather it may take nearly half a year.

To rid your pet of fleas, use a safe insect killer. As animals lick themselves, they sometimes swallow enough insecticide to make themselves sick. Cats do this more than dogs. Ask the advice of an animal doctor when it comes to waging war against the tough-shelled flea.

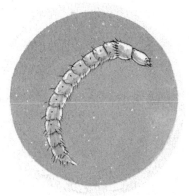

Bed Bug

Here is a bug that is truly a bug. Scientists set true bugs apart because of the type of beak or mouth parts they have for sucking blood or plant juices. You have to be a scientist with a microscope to study this proboscis. The rest of us don't want to see a bed bug at all.

A century ago, few people escaped meeting bed bugs. Fortunately, modern insect killers have brought them under control. In the United States and Canada, and the rest of the world, they can live wherever there are warm-blooded animals on land.

If you should be unlucky enough to stay in a hotel room that has them, sleep with the lights on. Bed bugs are animals of the dark. If they have eaten recently, they probably won't bother you. But if they are hungry, even daylight may not keep them away.

The bed bug is flat. Its abdomen is roundish or oval, coming to a slight point at the rear end. The short, wingless thorax partly covers the head, from which an eye bulges out on each side. It has medium long antennae. Over all, this bug is not much more than an eighth of an inch long.

The proboscis swings back under the head when not in use. Sensing a warm-blooded body – mouse, bird, bat, or man – the hungry bed bug crawls onto it with a step usually too light to be felt. The bug swings its beak forward to feed.

The mandibles of bed bugs have become tiny spears, called stylets. They lie in a groove down the insect's lengthened lower lip, or labium. The stylets are so sharp that the host seldom feels them enter the skin.

As the bed bug pierces the body, saliva runs into the wound and keeps the blood from clotting. Fortunately, these bugs carry no serious diseases.

A newly hatched nymph will feed for less than five minutes. An older nymph takes longer to stuff its body, and an adult bed bug may eat for ten to fifteen minutes. When the insect bulges with blood, the host may begin to feel it.

Between meals, adult bed bugs hide for a week or two. At this time, the female glues a few eggs a day to the furniture, the wall, or the rug. In her lifetime, she lays about two hundred tiny whitish eggs. Each egg has a cap at one end.

In a week or so, the young bed bug is ready to hatch. It swallows the air inside the egg until its body swells and fills the shell. Then it forces fluids from its body into its head; the head swells against the cap of the egg and breaks it off.

The yellowish nymph looks like a small adult. It feeds as soon as it can find a victim. If it gets its fill, it need not eat again until it sheds its exoskeleton.

In five moults the nymph reaches the adult stage. The whole process takes four to six weeks. Between each moult, the nymph needs at least one good meal.

In about a year, a bed bug dies of old age. After becoming an adult, it can live nearly that long without eating if it has to. No wonder bed bugs were difficult to get rid of before the invention of modern insecticides.

Bed bugs secrete an oil with an unpleasant, sweetish odour. If many bugs occupy one place, the odour becomes noticeable.

Before man evolved, bed bugs probably lived mainly on bats. Bats never eat bed bugs, and it is the smelly oil that prevents them from doing so. When early humans started to live in caves, they attracted the insects. The bugs have gone on producing the oil but they no longer need its protection.

Annual Cicada

Buzz-ZUZZZ-zuzzz-ZUZZZ-zuzzz. In July and August, rasping, buzzy calls sound during the heat of the day. They swell and fade, over and over. Male cicadas are letting the silent females know where they wait for mating.

The males "sing" by vibrating organs in the thorax. The females hear through instruments on their abdomens. The adults must mate soon, as they have but a week or two to live.

After leaving the male, the female uses her knife-sharp ovipositor to slice open twigs or small branches. In each slit, she lays a few eggs, which produce nymphs in a week or so.

The young drop to the ground and burrow under the surface. For the next four or five years, annual cicada nymphs suck juices from plant roots. They moult many times and grow to be one of our largest insects, measuring almost two inches.

Each year some cicadas reach full size. Someone who did not know they had been growing for a few years under the ground thought that cicadas reached maturity in a year. He mistakenly called them "annual" cicadas.

Having left the ground, the nymph crawls up a tree trunk or post. There it digs its claws in firmly. Before long, the back of the exoskeleton splits open. The adult slowly crawls out, looking almost wingless. Sacs of fluid on its back expand into wings.

The adult cicada crawls or flies away. The thin exoskeleton remains behind until wind, rain, or a curious boy or girl knocks it down.

If you draw a line from San Francisco Bay to the western tip of Lake Superior, you will find most annual cicadas south and east of the line. In Canada, they live from Lake Superior north through Ontario to James Bay and in most of Quebec and the Maritime Provinces.

When the first settlers landed in North America, they called these insects locusts. Actually, the cicadas are closer relations of bugs than of grasshoppers. They have jointed beaks with which they pierce and suck, much as bed bugs do. However, the beak of a bed bug attaches to the front of the face, while that of a cicada attaches to the underside of the head.

A cicada's head is short and wide, with a compound eye at each upper corner. Between the two main eyes are three small ones, which have only one lens apiece. These simple eyes are known as ocelli and are difficult to see because of their small size.

The thorax is wide, but the cicada's abdomen tapers rapidly to a point. Over the abdomen, the wings form a short ridge and slope down like the sides of a tent. The wings are so transparent you can easily see the body through them.

The front wings are much longer than the back pair. They extend well beyond the end of the abdomen. The heavy wing veins are greenish, and the insect's blackish body is also marked with green.

Where many cicadas live together, they injure trees. The egg slits weaken small branches and the wind blows them off. Fruit trees in particular are susceptible to damage.

Usually, the cicada's natural enemies keep it under control. In the eastern half of the United States, it is attacked by a large wasp known as a cicada-killer. The cicada also falls victim to blackbirds, grackles, sparrows, hawks, and gulls.

The cicada's song often sounds as if it is some distance from where the insect actually sits. If you try to find a cicada by its song, don't be surprised if it isn't there.

Spittlebug

Seeing a newly hatched spittlebug nymph, you might think it is having a bubble bath. Really, it is building a hideaway. Once it covers itself with foam, the hot sun will not dry it out and birds will not feed on it. You are more likely to see a weed coated with the froth than to see the nymph itself.

The nymph is a tiny green insect with a broad abdomen. Because its broad end makes it look somewhat frog-like and because adult spittlebugs hop from leaf to leaf, these insects are also called froghoppers. The foam has been given such crazy names as frog spit, cuckoo spit, and snake spit.

The bubbles are not spit at all. They are partly digested plant sap mixed with a material similar to that used by some other insects for spinning silk cocoons. The spittlebug nymph produces this slimy fluid from the opening at the end of its abdomen through which it excretes wastes. Also at the end of the abdomen, the nymph has tubes through which it can take in or push out air. By producing the slippery fluid and blowing out air at the same time, the nymph makes bubbles. It uses its feet and tail to spread the froth around itself and the stem or leaf on which it will feed.

From early summer, when it hatched, to mid or late summer, the young green spittlebug hides in its bubble palace. After several moults it crawls forth as a dull brown adult, though a few light brown to yellowish marks on the abdomen add a bit more colour.

By this time, the spittlebug has grown to be a fourth to a third of an inch long. It is very small when compared with an annual cicada. Yet you would probably notice some similarities and guess they are relatives.

The wings slope down the sides of the abdomen like a tiny roof and are transparent. The spittlebug seldom flies, but hops instead. Its leaping may attract your attention, for it seems restless and moves frequently. This also brings it to the attention of hungry birds.

The spittlebug has a broad head and thorax, but the abdomen does not taper like that of the cicada. Sometimes the spittlebug will be nearly as wide as it is long. The sucking mouth parts and the very short thin threads that serve as antennae resemble those of its large relative, but between its two compound eyes the spittlebug has two simple ones rather than three.

Late in summer, the female lays her eggs. She may

push them into a plant stem, or place them in the pocket formed where a leaf grows out of a stem.

If many nymphs hatch in one area, they can kill plants or branches by sucking the juices. They particularly injure pine trees, garden vegetables, strawberries, alfalfa, clover, and sometimes grapes.

Wherever you live in the United States and Canada, go for a walk in meadows or pine woods and look for the clumps of foam. When you find them, you can play detective. Some scientists say the adult female froghopper covers her eggs in a globe of froth. Others say only the nymphs produce the bubbles to cover themselves. If you scrape some of the foam away with a stick, you will be able to find out if there is a nymph inside or if there are eggs.

If there is nothing, a nymph has probably matured and hopped away. Look into many spittle sites before you reach your final opinion. Which will it be? Always nymphs, or sometimes eggs?

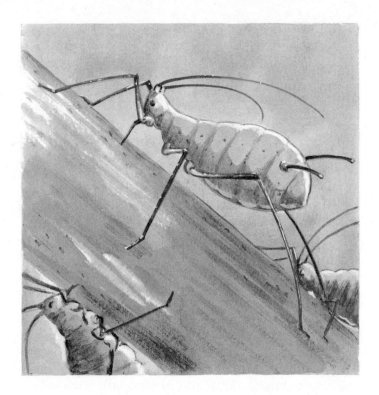

Aphid

Where juicy plants grow, aphids feed on them. You can find aphids on beans, peas, cabbages, melons, corn, grapes, roses, chrysanthemums, and trees such as pine, apple, peach, orange, and grapefruit.

Dozens of them on one plant can cause the leaves to curl and die. They also spread diseases from one plant to another.

Helping the gardener, farmer, and tree grower fight aphids are some insects and many birds. Ladybugs eat aphids. Green lacewings feed on the aphid so regularly they are called aphid lions. One wasp lays its eggs in an aphid nymph's body. When the wasp larvae hatch, they devour the aphid alive. Chickadees, flycatchers, and warblers feed regularly on aphids.

With so many enemies, how do aphids thrive? For one thing, they are difficult to see because of their colour and small size. Many nymphs and adults are greenish and blend with plant stems. Some that live on dark plants may be black or red. A full-sized adult is less than a quarter of an inch long, and nymphs are much shorter.

Like its relatives the cicada and the spittlebug, the aphid, or plant louse, sucks plant juices. When certain aphids do this, the plant behaves in a strange way. It grows a gall, or swelling, that covers and hides the insect.

In addition, aphids receive protection from certain ants. From its abdomen, an aphid discharges a sweet liquid known as honeydew. Many flies, bees, wasps, and ants eat this, and the ants care for the aphids in order to have a supply of it. The ants carry the aphids underground on chilly or stormy days. They transport aphid nymphs from one plant to another, making it possible for the young to have plenty of fresh food.

If an aphid fails to supply enough honeydew, the ants stroke the nymph with their antennae. This has been compared to milking, so aphids are often called ant cows.

At summer's end, a female that has mated with a male lays shiny black eggs. The eggs pass the winter stuck to the plants on which the nymphs will feed. They hatch in spring, and all the nymphs are females. Unlike the nymphs of most insects, they grow up to be wingless and can produce young without mating.

These wingless females do not lay their eggs but hold them in their bodies. The eggs hatch inside the adults and the nymphs are born fully formed. They too become wingless females and bring forth more nymphs – a new generation – in the same way.

If all these aphids remained on one plant, they would kill it and face starvation. But ants move some aphids, and now and again some nymphs become winged females that fly to other plants.

It takes about a week for a new generation of young to be produced, so several generations can result from each egg that hatches in the spring. In the north there may be six or eight generations, and in the warm south new generations may be produced all year round. On the average, there are a dozen generations a summer.

Finally, as fall arrives, many females with wings appear. These lay eggs from which develop both winged females and winged males. Mating occurs, and the eggs are laid that will survive the winter. Frost kills all the living aphids, but warm days the following spring start the cycle over again.

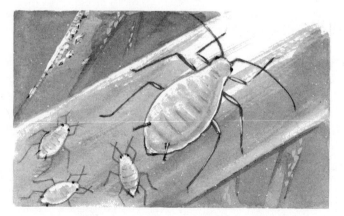

Dragonfly

The dragonfly has four wings. Therefore, it is not a true fly.

Most common in Canada and the United States is the green dragonfly. In southern Alaska, across southern Canada, and on south it makes its home. Look for it around ponds, quiet streams, swampy areas, and even damp meadows.

You will have no trouble seeing it for it is about two and a half inches long. More than half the length is the long, thin abdomen. Its thorax is green but the abdomen will be bluish and its transparent wings may also have a bluish look.

The head of the dragonfly appears to be all eyes. These large organs, which meet in the middle of the head, have about 30,000 lenses.

Approaching a fly, midge, gnat, or mosquito, the green dragonfly holds its thin legs like a net. Long hairs on the legs add to the basket effect, and in this the dragonfly catches its prey. It shoots out its hooked underlip, or labium, and sinks it into the victim's body. The dragonfly eats its meal on the wing with its sharp mandibles.

Most of the time, the dragonfly helps man by catching flying pests. From dawn till dark, the dragonfly hunts. For brief periods it rests on plants. When it does so, it holds its narrow wings out to the sides. On the wing, the dragonfly is one of the fastest insects in the world. Despite its speed, it is caught by some birds.

Unlike many insects, dragonflies migrate. Adults fly north in the spring, mate and lay their eggs, and then die. The following year, the eggs hatch and reach maturity, and in about August they move south. Studies need to be made as to whether moving helps them to have longer lives.

Dragonflies mate on the wing. The female then seeks plants standing in water. With her tough ovipositor, she sticks her eggs into a plant's stem just above the water line or just under it.

The long, thin eggs soon hatch and the young sink to the bottom of the pool. These nymphs, called naiads, are food for fish, ducks, and herons.

The naiads eat swimming larvae, such as those of mosquitoes, and may even catch small tadpoles and minnows. A naiad will live under water during one winter. It walks about or drives itself forward with jets of water from its breathing organs.

To breathe, a naiad draws water into gills at the rear of its abdomen. With its gill organs, it can separate oxygen from the water. It can squirt the water out of its gills with some force. This sends it shooting rapidly about the pool.

It takes about fifteen moults for a dragonfly to become an adult. For its final moult, a naiad climbs a plant into the air.

Once free of the last shell, the dragonfly dries for a day or two. You can easily catch it at this time. You will see that the wings have a thick network of veins. You will also find that the mandibles can give a painful nip, though they will do you no harm. Once it starts to fly, a dragonfly is hard to catch.

Giant Water Bug

How big is a giant? Among land mammals, the elephant might be called a giant. A blue whale is a giant mammal of the sea. The ostrich is a giant bird, and the crocodile a giant reptile. Fortunately insects, even "gigantic" ones, come in much smaller sizes than the other animals.

The giant water bug is common throughout the United States and in the southern parts of Canada. It reaches a length of about two inches and a width of half an inch. Among true bugs it is the largest you will see, as well as being one of the largest insects of any kind.

Besides being big, this water bug is strong. It is probably even stronger than the praying mantis. Not only does it grasp and eat other water insects, but also snails, frogs, tadpoles, small fish, and small water snakes.

On occasion, it will grasp something too big for it to hold. This may be because its large, bulging eyes are weak. Many other insects have better eyes. But if the giant water bug holds on long enough to swing its labium out from under its head and thorax, its bite may overcome the victim. It injects a poison that kills small creatures and may subdue larger ones.

For this reason, you will be wise to watch giant water bugs without trying to handle them. They can draw blood and cause you severe pain. Swimmers who have been bitten dread this bug and call it the toe-biter.

Ponds, lakes, and other quiet fresh waters serve as home for the giant water bug. Its middle and hind legs are long, flattened, and hairy and are used to propel the flat, brownish body zigzagging through the water.

The giant water bug's front legs, also flattened, remain ready to catch prey. Bent and poised at the sides of the head, they look like a pair of pincers.

Besides swimming, the bug can crawl on the bottom and even leaves the water to fly about. Most of the time its brown wings lie across one another over the back. But warm summer nights seem to turn this swimming insect into a flying traveller.

Night birds catch it when it ventures out of the water, and ducks and other water birds feed on it. Medium-size to large-size fish also gobble it down.

The adults mate under water. The females, which are larger than the males, seek plant stems below the surface on which to lay their eggs. These small white globes soon hatch, if they are not discovered by fish and ducks. The nymphs, looking much like adults except that they are smaller and wingless, crawl along the mud bottom catching larvae and other small water insects.

In China, where relatives of our giant water bug may reach a length of four inches, these insects are eaten as food in stews or soups. In North America, Indians of some tribes also eat these bugs. Foods and customs differ, just as "giants" do.

Backswimmer

Have you ever seen a water bug that looked something like a row-boat with six paddles? This relative of the giant water bug swims on its back. The three pairs of legs stretched out to the sides look a bit like oars, but two of the pairs seldom help the bug row.

The hind legs push the backswimmer through the water. They are longer and flatter than the other two pairs and many hairs grow along them. When the insect makes a swimming stroke, the hairs stand out and press against the water. As the bug folds its legs to pull them up for another stroke, the hairs lie flat and cause little resistance.

The front legs grasp the larvae, small insects, tadpoles, and little fish on which the backswimmer feeds. The middle legs help hold the victim. Like the giant water bug, the backswimmer has a poisonous bite but its venom is mild. If a backswimmer bites you, you will probably get an itchy swelling similar to a bee sting.

The female backswimmer sticks her eggs to plants or pushes them into particularly soft stems. They hatch in about a week, and the nymphs look like adults except that they are smaller and lack wings.

The young eat the same food as the adults, but capture smaller victims. Both nymphs and adults lie almost motionless in the water, looking toward the surface with their two bulging, compound eyes. When something of the right size passes overhead, they float up and grab it.

Because its belly is dark brown, with perhaps greyish or greenish markings, the backswimmer blends with the colour of the bottom of the pond when an animal looks down at it. Its back is light brown to yellowish or speckled white and brown. To an animal passing below, such as a fish, the backswimmer blends with the air above.

In spite of its colouring, the backswimmer falls prey to fish, water birds, and the giant water bug. Since it lives in the same areas as the giant water bug, it must always be on the watch for its large relative.

When fully grown, the backswimmer reaches a length of half an inch. On warm nights in midsummer, it may take to the air. Since it flies right side up, it must first turn over. It pops up out of the water, flips over, and lands on its belly before spreading its wings and taking off.

In summer, the backswimmer spends more time at the surface of the water. It rests there at an angle, with part of its abdomen in the air and its head under the water. While the backswimmer is at the surface, bubbles collect among the fine hairs on its belly. These oily hairs repel water, allowing the bug to carry the bubbles down into the water. They look like a coating of silver on its belly.

Under water, the backswimmer breathes the air in the bubbles. Also, the bubbles draw oxygen from the water, which freshens the imprisoned air for breathing. As a result, the backswimmer can rest below the surface for several hours.

When the backswimmer rows itself about or struggles with a victim, it rapidly uses the air supply in its bubbles. It must come to the top more often than if it were resting.

A thin film of ice on the pond does not harm backswimmers. They remain active, breathing air trapped under the ice. A thick coat of ice, however, sends them to the bottom to hibernate.

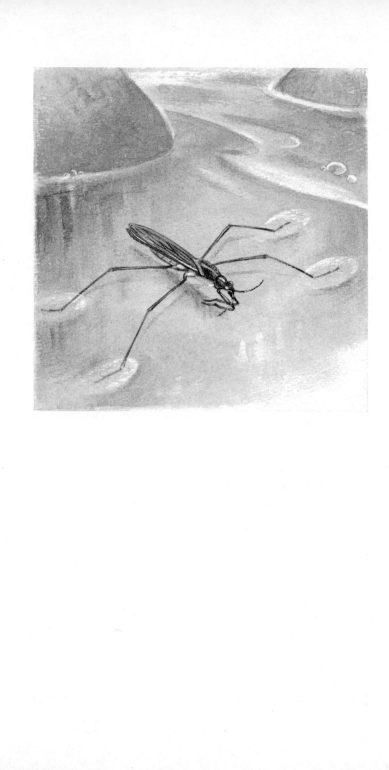

Water Strider

Try floating a needle in a glass of water. It can be done if you are careful. Water has surface tension, as if a thin film of water particles on the top were stuck together more tightly than the particles below.

Surface tension allows some lightweight animals to walk across ponds, lakes, and streams. One water bug that can do this is known as the water strider, or water skater, since it appears to slide rather than stride. It is one of the swiftest members of this branch of the bug family.

Fish and water birds catch the strider. It, in turn, hunts small insects that fall into the water or that it finds on water plants. Unlike giant water bugs, backswimmers, and others of its relatives, it eats dead creatures. Most bugs seek living food.

Although nearly as long as the backswimmer, the water strider weighs less because of its thinner body and legs. The short front legs, used for grasping prey, grow well forward on the thorax. The long, very thin middle and hind legs are attached near the rear. Since the strider has an unusually long thorax – about half its length – the middle and hind legs are near its middle.

The water strider holds its back four legs almost straight out to the sides, hardly bending the joints. It thereby spreads its weight over a relatively large area.

The ends of the running legs are covered with tiny hairs. These hairs spread out over the surface like snow shoes, giving the strider more area on which to stand. At the same time, hairs on the belly also keep the bug from sinking. All these hairs have a thin coat of oil, which does not mix with water.

When you try to float a needle in a glass, draw it between your fingers and see if the natural oils from your skin make it float more readily. Or grease it with a speck of lard, butter, or cooking oil.

The middle pair of legs do most of the work in moving the strider about. The rear pair provides balance and does the steering.

A water strider folds the leg hairs against its legs when it flies, so that it is not slowed down by their resistance to the wind. It flies less than some other water bugs and it is not a strong flyer. If it has wings, they are short, and many of these bugs lack wings altogether.

If its old pool dries up during a rainless summer, the

strider finds the nearest rock or log. It crawls under it to await the return of wetter days. As winter approaches, it hibernates.

The female pushes her eggs into a soft plant stem or glues them in batches to stems, always under water. The nymphs look like small adults without wings. When grown, they have large eyes and short antennae.

The water strider's back is dull brown to black, while its belly is whitish. Like the backswimmer, it may go unnoticed by a duck looking down on it or a fish looking up.

Most striders will be found east of the Rockies. They thrive in mild to cool climates, so you will not find as many in the southern United States as you will in the central and northern parts. In Canada, look for them in southern Manitoba, southern and central Ontario and Quebec, and the Maritimes.

Striders can be found in nearly every pool or stream in the countryside and sometimes they can be found skimming around on pools in city parks. Unlike giant water bugs and backswimmers, striders do not bite man.

Springtail

Arm yourself with a magnifying glass when you hunt for springtails. Although you can see their yellowish, greyish, or bluish bodies with the unaided eye, you can tell little about them. Look for ways in which these tiny animals differ from other insects.

The abdomen has six segments instead of eleven. On the back of the thorax there is no bump or mark of any sort to show that the ancestors of springtails once had wings. In other wingless insects, some mark or ridge indicates that wings once existed.

The springtail continues shedding its exoskeleton when it becomes an adult. True insects are through with moulting once they reach maturity. Some scientists say springtails are not really insects.

Hunt for springtails throughout the United States and Canada. The only place where they do not live is in deserts. These little leapers require moisture, and where the ground remains damp all year you may discover millions of them on one acre of land.

A springtail will usually be less than an eighth of an

inch long. Some species have bulb-shaped bodies, but others have abdomens that are more long and rounded, like cylinders. For its size, the springtail has long antennae. It also has eight simple eyes on each side of its head, but they lie so near each other that they look like one eye.

Below the abdomen grow unusual organs. One of these, near the front, looks like a tiny straw. Properly called a ventral (underside) tube, it more often goes by the name of "glue peg". The moisture at the end of this tube allows the springtail to stick itself to whatever surface it is on. Recent research shows that the tube also serves to draw moisture into the body.

At its rear end, the springtail has two long, thin organs that curve under the body and usually join near the base. These give the animal its spring. When not in use, two other organs, which can be called the catch, hold the springing organs up off the ground. If the catch lets go, the springing organs swing down and back, hurling the springtail up and forward. It may land eight inches away, but most species in North America only jump three to six inches.

Those that hop about on snow are called snow fleas. Springtails also travel on water. When doing so, they must watch out for water bugs and fish. On land they are eaten by mites and especially ants.

Many springtails wear a coat of minute scales.

These flake off easily. If caught by an ant or in a spider web, the springtail may wriggle loose and bound away unharmed. Springtails with hairy bodies have more difficulty escaping enemies.

For their own food, the springtails eat young plants and fungi. With their chewing mouth parts, they grind food before swallowing it.

A female will be larger than the male of her species. At mating time, he runs or hops around her, stands in her way, "whips" her with his antennae, and rubs his antennae against hers. They do not come in contact to mate. The male drops fluid on the ground, and the female's abdomen comes in contact with this.

The eggs, placed singly or in small groups under damp leaves or logs, absorb moisture and swell. In a matter of hours the outside shell breaks open, but a thin inner coat protects the young for a few days. When it hatches, it looks like an adult except that it is smaller.

Springtails in your damp basement, kitchen, or bathroom will do no damage. Outdoors, they are relatively harmless unless hundreds of them attack very young plants.

Caddisfly

Darkness falls. From under leaves beside streams, moth-like insects appear. A group gathers over the water and flies up, down, and around as if they are dancing.

These male caddisflies court the females with their zigzag flight. The females flutter out over the water, where mating takes place. The male has fulfilled his purpose in life. He probably will not eat again, and perhaps has never eaten since becoming an adult. Soon he will die, having lived a mature life for three or four weeks.

The female settles on a rock or plant in the stream. Females of some species crawl under the water to lay their eggs, but most put only their ovipositors beneath the surface.

The eggs often form a long strip, held together by a glue-like substance. Some females lay about three hundred eggs, but other species may lay a thousand.

In a few days an egg hatches, and the caddisworm, or larva, sinks to the bottom. A thick, dark skin covers its head and thorax, but its abdomen looks soft and white. It sets about building a case to protect that abdomen.

Depending on its species, a caddisworm uses sand, bits of leaves, twigs, or other material for its "house". It glues the pieces together with sticky silk from organs in its mouth until it has a solid tube in which to live.

When in danger, a larva pulls its head and thorax into its case. Danger comes mainly from fish, tough water bugs, and muskrats. Its enemies must break the case, for the larva holds itself in by hooks on the end of its abdomen.

Some caddisworms feed on small, soft plants. Others catch tiny larvae and other living creatures to eat. The hunters usually do not build cases, as these make them too slow.

Hunting caddisworms frequently spin funnels or nets of silk. The flow of the stream carries tiny animals into these nets. The hunters grasp their prey with strong front legs, which are the legs the "house" builders use in their construction work.

Winter finds the caddisfly still in the larval stage. Because it has gills on its abdomen and can draw oxygen from the water directly into its body, the larva can live under ice.

When it moults, the caddisworm crawls out of its case. This happens six or eight times during its nine or ten months as a larva. After shedding, it builds a larger house or adds an addition to the front of the old one.

To pupate, the larva anchors its case to a rock and closes the front with silk. Then it spins a cocoon around itself and after two or three weeks chews its way out.

It crawls or swims to the surface and pulls itself up a plant stem to shed its final pupal exoskeleton. Its dull brown to yellowish body makes it difficult to see in the dark but it is caught by bats and nighthawks. When it flies low over water, trout leap to catch it.

If it eats at all, the adult caddisfly feeds on nectar. While eating or resting, its hairy wings slope like those of the cicada.

The nearest relative to the caddisfly is probably the moth. However, some caddisflies have long antennae, even longer than the body, which moths do not. Also, the proboscis of the caddisfly is short and straight instead of long and coiled.

Look for caddisflies near streams, ponds, and lakes. They can be found from the southernmost part of the United States to the northernmost part of Canada, and from the east coast to the west.

Lacewing

Stand near a bright street lamp at night to hunt for lacewings. Although lacewings appear before dark, they do most of their slow, weak flying at night. Notice the four thin, filmy green or brown wings, which spread an inch or less from tip to tip. You will not be surprised to know that this frail-looking insect has trouble escaping bats, night birds, beetles, and sand flies.

The young lacewing falls prey to the larvae of certain flies and to a wasp that lays her egg in its pupal case. But enough lacewings survive to help control the aphid population. The larvae bite into aphids with slicing mandibles to drain their victims' juices. Other food consists of mealybugs and scale insects.

The two largest groups of lacewings in North America are the brown and the green lacewings. The green, with a length of half an inch or just over, live throughout the United States and Canada except for the far north. The smaller brown lacewings occur mainly in southeastern Canada, in the eastern United States, and in the woods of British Columbia.

Green lacewing larvae practise camouflage. After draining aphids, the lacewing sticks some of the aphid exoskeletons onto its spiny hairs. It may add other debris until it looks like a six-legged trash pile. It escapes the eyes of its enemies and slips up on victims more easily than it might otherwise be able to do. Both brown and green lacewing larvae, being swift, can overtake aphids, but it is the ants they must fear. Where ants are tending aphids in order to "milk" them, soldier ants will fight intruders.

After ten to twelve days of eating, the lacewing larva spins itself into a silky, pea-sized globe. Most species of lacewings hibernate during the winter in this tiny globe.

In spring, the lacewing bites its way free of the cocoon and crawls a short distance. Its pupal skin breaks, the many-veined wings expand, and the adult starts eating aphids. It eats far less than it did as a youth.

In the summer, the female mates. In order to lay eggs, certain species of lacewings must work very hard. For each egg, the female touches her abdomen to a leaf and drops a gluey substance onto it. As the cement hardens, she lifts her tail in order to stretch the sticky material into a thin stalk. She then places an egg on top of the stalk. She must go through the same operation about six hundred times.

The stalk holds the egg for a week until the young cut out of their shells. The newly hatched larvae remain on top of the stalks while their bodies dry. Then they slide or drop down onto a leaf. If any lacewing eggs near by stand on stalks that are too short, the newly hatched larvae will devour them.

Many lacewings have shiny coppery or red-gold eyes. These insects are often called golden-eyes.

If you approach a lacewing, it may play dead. It is wisest to leave it alone. It can produce a skunky liquid that leaves an unpleasant odour even if you wash your hands several times.

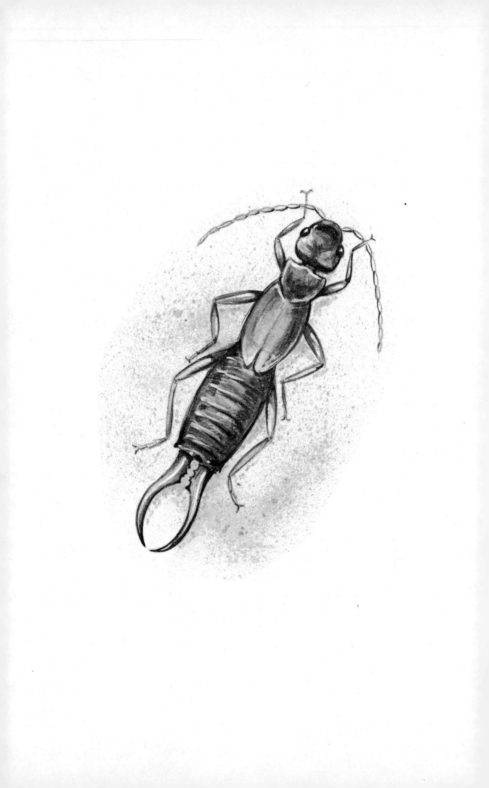

Earwig

No one knows for sure how the earwig got its strange name, but there was an old superstition that these animals would crawl into people's ears. This, of course, is not true.

Earwigs hide under bark and leaves, and in the cracks of old wooden buildings, especially in damp places. Their flattish bodies slip into very small crevices. At night they crawl forth to feed on the bodies of dead insects and rotting vegetation. Some capture live prey, if it is small and slow enough for them to overtake. Soft plant stems, flower petals, and pollen also provide them with food.

If you find one in the house, do not be alarmed. It will do no damage. Only if you live in the area north of Canada and Alaska are you likely to be out of earwig territory. Most species live along the coasts, especially near the Gulf of Mexico and the Pacific.

Our largest earwigs reach a length of just over half an inch, while smaller species may be only a quarter of an inch long. Most are dark, being reddish brown to black. Even if you lack a magnifying glass, you will notice that certain features stand out.

At the tip of its abdomen, the earwig has two hook-like organs. These look a bit like a pair of tweezers or like miniature ice tongs. They are called cerci. Although the earwig may receive vibrations through its cerci, it also uses them in its defence. If you pick up an earwig, it will give you a nip with its tweezers. It has no poison and probably will not be strong enough to break the skin, but you will feel it. Some species use the tweezers for folding and tucking the wings out of sight.

When not in use, the flying wings lie folded under the front wings. The front ones are really leathery shields and barely cover the thorax. Since the rear wings are much longer, they must fold to fit under the front ones. They fold in pleats from side to side like a fan, and from back to front. When they have been tucked under the front covers, only a small part sticks out. Earwigs seldom fly and you may find species that have no wings at all.

The earwig has a heart-shaped or oval head. You can see its two medium-sized compound eyes easily, but the single-lens ocelli are not noticeable and some species do not have them. The antennae, half the length of the body, look like strings of beads.

Except in the Gulf Coast area, a female usually

114

lays one batch of eggs each summer. She stands guard over them until they hatch in a few days, and some mothers also guard the nymphs for a day or two. Once the young crawl from the nest beneath the soil or under debris on top of the ground, she has nothing more to do with them.

The nymphs look like small, wingless adults. After four to six moults, which take only a few weeks, they will be full grown. Like the mature earwigs, the young produce a fluid from their abdomens that smells like tar. This helps protect them, though they are still caught by night-flying birds and beetles.

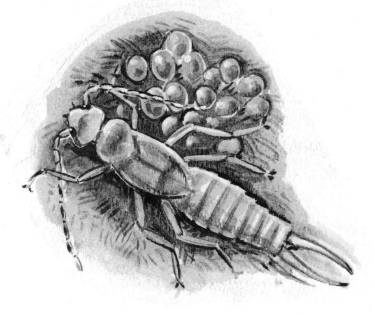

Silverfish

You will have more luck hunting silverfish indoors than outside. Look in damp cellars and around old books or old stocks of newspapers. Wherever there are buildings, from the southern United States to central Canada, you can find these silvery grey to greenish white insects slipping silently around kitchen and bathroom pipes and across basement floors.

Some species live outdoors, where they eat dry or rotting leaves. But it is easier to observe those that share our houses. Indoors, they eat the paste from behind wall paper, the glue that holds covers on books, and the starch in your clothing. A silverfish will eat paper as well.

Silverfish have been in this world longer than any other living insects, as far as we know. They have changed little from the way they were millions of years ago. We call them primitive insects. They remain a link between the ancient animals from which today's insects developed and the modern insects themselves.

Shaped like a half-inch-long dagger blade, the

silverfish has a broad front thoracic segment and then it tapers, section by section, to the tip of its abdomen. No wings exist to hide the back, which looks silvery because of a coating of tiny scales. These scales rub off easily, which helps the insect to escape from hungry ants.

The head has a small compound eye on either side, or no eyes at all. Long, somewhat feathery antennae guide the silverfish. The mouth is made up of two chewing palps.

There are three long, feathery feelers at the rear of the abdomen. Two stick out to the sides and are related to the cerci of modern insects. A third sticks straight back, and these can all be moved just as the front antennae can.

You will not have much luck handling silverfish. Their flattish bodies have a soft skin rather than a tough exoskeleton, so they are easily injured. To escape their enemies, such as ants, beetles, and man, they run swiftly.

Besides the usual six legs, a silverfish has stubs along its belly. Scientists believe these are the remains of other legs, which this primitive insect has lost through the centuries. This shows that the silverfish may be one of the links between the development of many-legged animals like centipedes and the true six-legged insects.

The female silverfish lays one, or a few, tiny eggs at a time, hiding them in cracks and under wallpaper. The young soon hatch and look exactly like adults except for their small size. They shed their skins and grow larger.

By the time a female has moulted six to a dozen times, she has matured enough to lay eggs. This does not mean that she has become a full-sized adult. With true insects, only grown adults, which have moulted for the last time, can mate.

The female silverfish can moult again after laying her first eggs. Some time after her next moult, she will probably lay again, and then somewhat later she will shed again. It may be one or two years before she finally reaches full size, and she may have shed two to four dozen times.

During all this time she has continued to look exactly the same. Only her size has changed. It is no wonder some scientists find insects to be more fascinating than all other animals in the world.

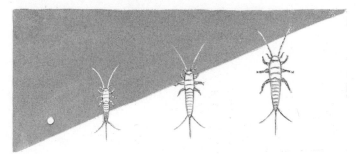